Where Dreams Are Created

Mary Etta Jones

Table of Contents

Reflections	3
If Only	4
Our Twilight Hours	5
Season of Life	6
Storm Rages	7
Tales Of Elfin Ways	8
The River Has Its Memories	9
They Thought Her Crazy	10
What Is This Muse	11
A World Away	12
Let Him Free	13
The Dragon And The Unicorn	14
His Song	15
A Christmas Alone	16
Ghost Trail	18
Yes Dear	19
Moors And Hinterlands	20
A World So Different	21
Where Memories Dwell	22
Contentment Of Love	23
Through The Night	24
Willing To Wait	25
White Wolves In Keep	26
Meant To Be	27
Within The Mind	28
A Hole In The Ocean Floor	30
Winters Wonderland	31
Why Do I Cry -a poem i wrote while caring for my mother-	32
Only Her Survival	33
Hello My World	34
Hello My World -continued-	35
Days Are Gone -for momma-who passed from alzheimers in 2004-	36
Fury -written by my granddaughter, Adrienne, at 13-	37
For Who I Am	38

Copyright: Mary Etta Jones 2011
All rights reserved

ISBN 978-0-615-55377-1

I am dedicating this book to the man in my life Fredrick A Jones Sr...the father of my sons...my lifetime companion...to the end.

Reflections

i sit here watching the fire...thinking
of life...what it means
wondering why we spend our lives
pleasing others
while we wither away into
nothingness...just to please
reflections of life always brings
questions with no answers

i try to add some humor to my
life...moments of gentleness
quiet serene moments...a quietness to
my life...i fail
there is always something that has to
be done...now
reflections of life always brings
questions with no answers

people who have to be satisfied...egos
sated...wants replied to
yet i find im not part of this...never
have been...never will be
im only a moment...my words not
important...my ideas less
reflections of life always brings
questions with no answers

fault is found with what is said...ears
occupied with the mind
so i here...contemplating...
wondering...what did i do wrong
only to be told im having a moment...
talk to me when it passes
reflections of life always brings
questions with no answers

If Only

dreams flow through my head of days
past
when youth could do no wrong...life
was good
the freedom felt...the acts performed...
were they wrong
how different life would have been...
if only i had known

things omitted in childhood...youth
in the dark
as life raced forward as a speeding
train out of control
and i asked...is there no end...
where is the light
how different life would have been...
if only i had known

actions perceived...ideas run
rampant...mind speeding on
falling into the traps only life seemed
to know about
continuing on as if nothing was
wrong...nothing at all
how different life wold have been...
if only i had known

i tried to put the brakes on...it broke
in my hands
i cried at the fear that rose within me
groping my way through life...
what is going on
how different life would have been...
if only i had known

Our Twilight Hours

when night falls...as we lay in our
beds...just before sleep overcomes
our minds wander into worlds we can
only imagine...thoughts flutter
seeing possibilities...of things to
come...of dreams that could be
our twilight hours of ideas...going on
ramparts within our heads

ideas we toy with...developing into
reality...then fall asleep to dream
how many have followed their
dreams...become their potential
is that where greatness comes
from...people we admire come from
our twilight hours of ideas...going on
ramparts within our heads

some follow those dreams...see
themselves doing what dreams told
never giving up or being afraid to give
it a chance...believing in themselves
becoming their dreams...whom they
want to be
our twilight hours of ideas...going on
ramparts within our heads

is this how heros are born...visualizing
a dream come true...never giving up
men and women...possessing the
ability to make dreams become reality
not afraid to try...ready to follow up
with a fantasy...to make it come alive
our twilight hours of ideas...going on
ramparts within our heads

Season of Life

the cornfields are all drying up...the
sun shines down
weather is changing...trees are
beginning to show some red
birds begin to take formation for the
trip southward
the twilight season of life

i feel a part of this change as i reach
that stage of my life
where youth is a memory of days past
and i now begin to reflect on purposes
the twilight season of life

the clouds cover the sky and darken
with winter storms brewing over the
horizon
the chill in the air reminds us what is
to come
the twilight season of life

i see myself changing with the seasons
now my hair is gray...wrinkles appear
overnight
and like the changing of time...i have
changed who i am
the twilight season of life

Storm Rages

i sit at the window contemplating the events of life
thunder peals in the background...as the rains pelts down
storms always put me in a reflective mood
as the storm rages...my thoughts begin to travel

wondering at the mysteries of my surroundings
can i ever understand why things happen as they do
why i dont have the control...why it isn't allowed to be
as the storm rages...my thoughts begin to travel

i then see others also have disquieting moments
i realize im not the only one...life is an upheaval
it is how we deal with it...how we learn from it
as the storm rages...my thoughts begin to travel

a lot of people fail to recognize this and flounder
some refuse to face it...others refuse to be flexable
but the truth is...it will always be there to tax us
as the storm rages...my thoughts begin to travel

Tales Of Elfin Ways

floating above my bed...was a little
elfin wizard
with a large book
his wizened face...long beard...and
sage smile...captavated my mind
with a puff on his pipe...he began to
speak of such tales for me
he greeted me with tales of elfin ways

each night he came...settled himself
comfortably...then lit his pipe
his eyes would begin to twinkle...as he
opened his book of intrigue
the elfin court was always famous for
such hilarious misdeeds
he greeted me with tales of elfin ways

i'd listen rapurously to his stories...
laughter following each tale
elfin youngsters who always seemed to
be in mischief of some kind
of their comical ways...of their serious
side...the elfin world intrigues
he greeted me with tales of elfin ways

he'd tell me of the care and love they
had for the forest and animals
how they balanced each other
out...how meticously the elves worked
their homes high in the
trees...sheltered by this lush branches
he greeted me with tales of elfin ways

just before i'd fall asleep...he'd take
his leave...with a promise to return
the thought of his pending return
always seemed to comfort me
he took his leave...then turn to me
saying..."dont lose your elfin ways"
he greeted me with tales of elfin ways

The River Has Its Memories

sitting on the shore of the river...i
watch the barges pass
they travel in either directions with
various destinations
there is a calming effect upon me as
soothing waves pass
the river has its memories...as do i

i think about what the river has
seen...the secrets it holds
as it slowly floats by me...i feel the
calls of past adventures
events of history...some
recorded...others unknown to us
the river has its memories...as do i

my mind tries to capture all the
essence i feel of past times
the loves...the losses...the miricles of
birth...even the sadness
lives this river has seen of days gone
past...millions of years
the river has its memories...as do i

my minds eye sees all the men and
women pass before me
with all their stories for me to
imagine...all to feel in my soul
i realize someday someone will add
me to the history
the river has its memories...as do i

They Thought Her Crazy

she danced around the room...a lonely
figure in the dark
dancing to a tune only she heard...only
she wished for
people would enter the room...shake
their heads...then walk away
they thought her crazy...only she knew
it was them

she had suffered much throughout her
life...yet she was happy
her world was filled with kindness and
love...all was hers
as she twirled a hand took hold of her
and began to dance with her
they thought her crazy...only she knew
it was them

surprise took hold of her...she turned
to face such beautiful eyes
he stared straight into her eyes and
soul...a smile upon his face

he held her close dancing to the tune
only they could hear
they thought her crazy...only she knew
it was them

their world expanded as each opened
doors for the other
they became a part of each
other...feeling what the other felt
the world began to filter
through...sunshing once more present
they thought her crazy...only she knew
it as them

they slowly migrated into the
world...retaining their own ideas
keep the world at bay...true to
themselves and what they perceived
knowing that they danced to a
different tune than others
they thought her crazy...only she knew
it was them

What Is This Muse

sometimes i wonder at the insistance
writing has become
then i begin to wonder why some are
touched... others are not
just where do these ideas and
inspirations come from
what is this muse all poets seem to live
with

as we work...play...or just live only to
be rudely interrupted
another inspiration has hit...must
write this down
to write it down lest we forget its
importance to the world
what is this muse all poets seem to live
with

ideas that seem to just pop into our
heads...where ever we may be
how any night are we
awakened...forced to write them down
or at the strangest places...to just sit
down amd madly write
what is this muse all poets seem to live
with

we are enslaved to this inconsiderate
master...who must be obeyed
this demanding...this invisible thing
that resides within our minds
demanding us to drop everything...
just to write to the world
what is this muse all poets seem to live
with

A World Away

upon yonder shores with soft swaying
trees...inviting beaches
of forested mountains...calling one
forth to investigate
waterfalls thousands of feet in
heighth...luscious ferns all around
in a world away from the cries of
everyday holocaust

pools of clear waters...begging you to
join in the warm cascades
lolling on a bed of fronds...gazing into
the skies...clouds floating by
no where to go...nothing to do...just
relax...enjoy the solitude
in a world away from the cries of
everyday holocaust

dreams filtering through the mind...
worries floating away
calm washes over your body...
drowiness takes over the mind
into the world of the sleeping mind...
where dreams rule the day
in a world away from the cries of
everyday holocaust

soft petals of fragrant flowers gently
brush your face...eyes open
the senses take in the aromas around...
as you deeply sigh
of a land far away...where dreams are
made the way you want
in a world away from the cries of
everyday holocaust

Let Him Free

deep within the soul of mankind lies a
dark shadow
one so evil even the angel tremble with
fear
he lies trapped within the recesses of
the mind of man
to let him free will destroy everything
we know and value

man has always carried this entity
locked securly away
but there have been extreme times
when this evil has escaped
these times have caused us much
anguish and terrors to our minds
to let him free will destroy everything
we know and value

think about all the horrors of history
we have seen or known
the demon within does exist know
him and weep...for he is us

we have caused the horrors that lives
amongst us by letting go
to let him free will destroy everything
we know and value

he will soon be in control and at the
helm of our future again
like hitler...hannibal...stalin...jack the
ripper...terrors of the mind
can we live through horrors like that
again...do we really want that
to let him free will destroy everything
we know and value

do we dare let him free...can we
prevent another holocaust
can we protect our world from
ourselves...do we care to even try
thought to ponder...just how
important is this world and ourselves
to let him free will destroy everything
we know and value

The Dragon And The Unicorn

the dragon sat complacently looking
at the unicorn as it grazed
"tell me little unicorn how your
golden horn upon your head doth
work?"
raising its head, chewing thoughtfully,
he finally turned to the dragon
wisdom comes to the dragon and the
unicorn as they talk

"a good question to ask oh mighty
dragon, but a harder one to answer"
the dragon looked confused thought
about it for awhile then asked another
"if it is hard to answer does that infer
that you are not sure yourself?"
wisdom comes to the dragon and the
unicorn as they talk

"yes, it is true, i know what it can do,
alas, i do not know how it is done"
totally abashed by the reply...he
picked up a bone and began to eat it
"it amazes me to think that something
that is a part of you is also unknown to
you"
wisdom comes to the dragon and the
unicorn as they talk

"it really doesnt bother, for i know it
works upon an evil thought and
destroys"
the dragon digested this bit of
information than placidly placed the
bone down
"well, little unicorn, i can see now that
i must control my evil thoughts
around you"
wisdom comes to the dragon and the
unicorn as they talk

the unicorn once again lowered his
head silently grazed in comfort
the dragon mulled this over staring at
the sky then slowly picked up his bone
never noticing the grin on the
unicorns mouth as he continued to
graze
wisdom comes to the dragon and the
unicorn as they talk

His Song

His Song

softly the song crept from his throat
a soft...beautiful...haunting sound
filling the air with a softness
my heart filled with the peace of his song

with a rush he let go of his joy
releasing his song to it fullest
all stopped to listen...hearts filling with awe
my heart filled with the peace of his song

A Christmas Alone

she stood upon the cliff alone...a
gentle breeze brushing her hair
her gaze watching intently for a ship
to appear...patiently waiting
a fear deep within her heart that it
would not appear in time
a christmas alone without her
love...the children missing him

the tree was all decorated...the
presents all wrapped and underneath
she had the plans all prepared for their
visits...christmas eve tidings
visits and gifts for the children in
orphanages...gifts for the infirm
a christmas without her love...the
children missing him

she knew the lonliness and fears of a
ships captains' wife
yet her love for him had surpassed
those disadvantages
their children accepting their
lives...anxious yet good natured
a christmas without her love...the
children missing him

she stood there gazing...the memories
of past christmas' flooding her mind
still the ships mast failed to
appear...apprehension gripping her
heart
there she stayed watching the horizon
year after year...hoping
a christmas without her love...the
children missing him

A Christmas Alone
-continued-

each year after that at christmas...the family continued their traditions
visiting orphanges, hospitals...tending the poor...always in his memory
keeping the joy of the holy day...knowing his spirit went with them
a christmas without her love...the children missing him

to this day on christmas eve...it is said...if you walk to the cliff
there you will see a lone woman in old fashioned attire...standing
waiting for her captain...reminding all of the deepness of love
a christmas alone without her love...the children missing him

Ghost Trail

riding hard...never ending
trail...always the same route
never ending...every night you hear
the pounding of hooves
no one in sight...just the constant
sound of many hooves
traveling the night on a long dusty
ghost trail

you know the history...you know the
stories recited
but it never prepares you for the
chaotic sounds you hear
the unnerving sounds of numerous
hooves running wild
traveling the night on a long dusty
ghost trail

you remember the stories about the
massive stampede
the thunderous night of men and
cattle running wild
the cattle spooked by a lightening
bolt...running mindlessly
traveling the night on a long dusty
ghost trail

men upon horses...racing to keep up
with the herd...to stay alive
one false move and they would be
trampled in the panic
praying this would soon end...having
it end with their deaths
traveling the night on a long dusty
ghost trail

Yes Dear

i chitter...i chatter...words..ideas...
come from my mouth
changes i want to make...things i want
us to do together
he sits...a befuddled look on his
face...then says...yes dear
our usual response now to keeping the
peace...yes dear

his time approaches when he think i
need a change in my life
this should go here...that should go
there...where can i put mine
i sit here with a pained expression on
my face...yes dear
our usual response now to keeping the
peace...yes dear

we spend time talking about our
coming adventures
he wants to go here...i want to go
there...where do we go
he suddenly looks at me...i suddenly
look at him...yes dear
our usual response now to keeping the
peace...yes dear

there is an adjustment to our lives...we
both agree
our personalities...our patterns
developed...styles adopted
we think about this...but when
voiced...all we can say is...yes dear
our usual response now to keeping the
peace...yes dear

Moors And Hinterlands

standing upon great boulders viewing the scene
of mountainous lands...vast lochs...green misty forest
inspiring magnificent majesties...this ancient land of mine
phantom dreams of misty moors and hinterlands

where histories are made...battles fought...kingdoms born
highlands of mysteries shrouded with prophecies proclaimed
a realm to behold...as time passes for all to see and love
phantom dreams of misty moors and hinterlands

dreams that see the future...people reaching towards the unknown
of past lives that dig deep within the heart and soul of men
visions of a land rooted where ancestors of past are honored
phantom dreams of misty moors and hinterland

futuer sons and daughters feeling the past...begging them to return
drawing their spirits to a homeland far away...drawing them back
a homeland only dreams can remember of scottish moors
phantom dreams of misty moors and hinterland

A World So Different

i see a world that frightens me...not like the one of the past
this one is self oriented...no time or patience for others
a world now of violence...of hate...of anger...of self
not like the world i came from...a world so different

i feel a world that makes me sad...that makes me so alone
one that no longer cares for the others in need
where people are discarded...become homeless
not like the world i came from...a world so different

i know a world that has made me untouchable
that turns its back on those like me...who live in fear
a world of fear...of itself...its neighbors...even its own families
not like the world i came from...a world so different

where people go on killing sprees...terrorism a normality
where the jobs and the economy generate more homeless
and families struggle each day just to survive
not like the world i came from...a world so different

Where Memories Dwell

of a time long ago...of memories that
never seem to fade
where dreams were made of
fantasy...reality pushed aside
as the mind traveled roads that were
made of nightmares
you live within the shadow
world...where memories dwell

tears fall with no recourse when the
minds terrors are awakened
of lives shattered...when delusions of
the mind took command
happiness becomes short lived...when
memory lane is visited
you live within the shadow
world...where memories dwell

wondering around...you try to come to
terms...try to accept the past
knowing they were necessary events
needed to grow upon
but the pain they caused...is
sometimes unbearable to remember
you live within the shadow
world...where memories dwell

wishing the pain was not necessary...
recognizing there was no other way
realizing past events cant be
changed...trying to accept what was
yet the pain of what was done...lives
on to always remind you
you live within the shadow
world...where memories dwell

Contentment Of Love

in the shadows of my mind i feel your touch
sensing your closeness...knowing you'll always be
even apart the security i feel is always there
my heart feels the contentment of love

i feel your arms around me whenever i stand alone
sitting in my chair i feel the gentle kiss upon my neck
i sense you everywhere...wherever...i am never alone
my heart feels the contentment of love

there are no words left to express the way i feel
i have used them all to tell you...yet the love remains
never leaving...never wavering...holding on so tightly
my heart feels the contentment of love

watching the moon at the window i think of you...of us
always together...never to be alone again...we are one
we have always been a one...we will always be a one
my heart feels the contentment of love

Through The Night

the wind blew in my face as i stood by
the shore
i felt the cold through my coat chilling
me to the bones
yet i stood there in deep
thought...trying not to remember
chilly breath showed through the
night...so did my heart

i had faced many hardships...many
difficult decisions
always wondering if my decisions
were the right ones
or would i learn to regret the choices i
made...so unsure
chilly breath showed through the
night...so did my heart

the weight of what i had decided was
heavy upon me
could i carry it through...would i even
dare...only time
time to know...time to learn...time to
find...find the truth
chilly breath showed through the
night...so did my heart

as the night came to pass...the sun
slowly rose...i turned
walked away from my life...hoping the
future would know
be gentle upon my heart and
soul...give me the strength
chilly breath showed through the
night...so did my heart

Willing To Wait

there is a dream out there...waiting for me
one that waits to be fulfilled...just for me
it doesnt matter my age...only time controls
dreams can come true for those willing to wait

i kept my dream close to my heart...never sharing
always being true to my destiny...never wavering
hoping i was on the right track...where my dream would be
dreams can come true for those willing to wait

i have learned most of my lessons...received my reward
still have more to learn...more to go...then maybe
my dream will be reached...but i am a patient one
dreams can come true for those willing to wait

wait my turn...while those ahead of me are fulfilled
i will feel pride for them...knowing how hard they worked
just like me...waiting for their dream to come true
dreams can come true for those willing to wait

White Wolves In Keep

White Wolves In Keep

'o' maid of avalon
watch o'er thy sword
nae allow wrong bearers near
with the white wolves in keep

keep thine watch steady
till thy rightful bearer appears
then turn o'er thine watch
with the white wolves in keep

Meant To Be

Meant To Be

hush child...do not fear
there is time for you to grow
to gain wisdom and strength
be the angel you were meant to be

time to see your surroundings
see the trying times there is
find your place to help it grow
be the angel you were meant to be

to grow and be the help only you can be
protect the innocent as only you are
hush child...do not fear
be the angel you were meant to be

Within The Mind

watching the rowboat get smaller...she
stood alone upon the warf
her anger subsiding...she knew her
mistake was her undoing
yet her mind still felt the fear...not sure
where it came from
spiralling within the mind were the
thoughts of accumulated fears

knowing she couldnt face the world
anymore as she perceived it
she climed the stairs to the deck and
collapsed upon the settee
sitting there quietly...absorbing the
sights and sounds...feeling the wind
spiralling within the mind were
thoughts of accumulated fears

she turned...walked up the hill to the
cabin...her retreat for healing
the solitude beconed her to join...the
serenity felt as she neared
the cabin was her haven...for an
injured mind that cried for healing
spiralling within the mind were the
thoughts of accumulated fears

as the breeze brushed gently against
her cheeks...she watched the water
water rippling...as a lone loon sailed
across...sounding his haunting cry
a doe gracefully walked to the waters
edge for a drink...as a buck watched
spiralling within the mind were
thoughts of accumulated fears

Within The Mind
-continued-

how her world had crumbled was confusing to her...
terrifying to her soul
she knew something was not right...she just didnt know
where to start
nor where her search would lead her...was her trust well
placed...she wondered
spiralling within the mind were thoughts of accumulated
fears

no matter...right now she had to heal...she had to rest...she
had to pull together
this island...on this lake away from the world...would give
her sanctuary for awhile
till once more her mind could function...face the
world...deal with the collapse
spiralling within the mind were thoughts of accumulated
fears

A Hole In The Ocean Floor

down below the ocean floor...lays a
hole spewing oil
at a depth no man has ever tried
before nor can control
oil gushing deep within the
water...one that kills and destroy
a hole within the ocean floor that
never should have been

lies told to mask mistakes...actions
taken to hide guilts responsible
where is the valor...the trust of the
world...now the carelessness survives
lack of regard for the safety of this
world...the trust of all ignored
a hole within the ocean floor that
never should have been

marine life dies...wetlands that shrivel
away...dreams disappearing
peoples lives alter...as lifestyles come
to an end...hopes die
ones they trusted...allowed greed to
take control...judgments fade
a hole within the ocean floor that
never should have been

where does it end...where does it
begin...are there any answer at all
can the damage be redeemed...can the
destruction be healed
is the trust now lost forever as
desperation to repair bears out
a hole within the ocean floor that
never should have been

Winters Wonderland

gazing out the window...watching the snow cascade down
roads...sidewalks...even the grass...slowly begin to disappear
everything around me...becomes a pristine blanket of snow
the winters wonderland envelops my world

i watch transfixed...as the world becomes a sparkling ice palace
trees bend from the weight of icicles...as snow falls
sighing at the complete silence that allows the mind to travel
winters wonderland envelops my world

i have waited for this day...when the magic of winter is born
seeing the purity of snow on the first day of a hard snowfall
fills my mind with wonder and awe for this glorious vision
the winters wonderland envelops my world

it is becoming daylight as a cardinal flies to a nearby icy branch
red feathers standing out in contrast...the beauty breathtaking
the sadness returns once more...as a car slides down the street
winters wonderland envelops my world

Why Do I Cry
-a poem i wrote while caring for my mother-

my sadness reaches a plateau i never knew existed
i walk down the street looking at everything and nothing
i see the beauty most take for granted and i cry
i no longer have the ability to control my emotions
why do i cry...maybe i cry at the loss of myself

i see so much more than i use to...i want to know more
my mind goes from one to another...analyzing as i go
i want to know so much and cram it all in
i cant see enough anymore and i cry at the beauty
why do i cry...maybe i cry at the loss of myself

life is short...when you hear alzheimers...it becomes shorter
you want to learn about alzheimers... but your kinda frightened
you watch loved ones turn away from you...it hurts so
your friends stop coming by or calling...you ask yourself...why
why do i cry...maybe i cry at the loss of myself

i wish time could be reversed...i know it isnt so
i wish a cure would be found...again i know it isnt so
but mostly i wish people understood... i know it isnt so
so i guess its up to me to try and set the record straight
why do i cry...maybe i cry at the loss of myself

Only Her Survival

she hangs in the balance of life...
sanity on a thread
her world only a dream...
pain has pushed her hard
a world she created from the dust
of dispair
only her survival is real

life was hard...sometimes cruel
lessons unbearable
yet she hangs on to life...
a cold lonly existance
misunderstood by many...
abandoned...pushed aside
only her survival is real

mistakes have been many...
only hurts continue to flare
she feels the unforgivness...
falls deeper into her retreat
trust of others now lost...
trust in self now gone
only her survival is real

still she attempts her escapes from her
self imposed prison
a careless word...sends her running
back to her safety
cam she leave her fantasy world...
will she accept who she is
only her survival is real

Hello My World

tears begins to slowly fall...my mind is
in another place
one filled with anguish and pain...why
am i here again
i dont want to be here...it hurts too
much...please go away
hello my world...i see your back again

there use to be a time when they lived
deep inside me
tucked away nice and neat...where no
one saw them...or knew
hidden away...i was like an iceberg
...no feelings...no visible pain
hello my world...i see your back again

i have no control over these
emotions...they wont go away
i used to be able to hide them...look
the other way...deny them
no more...they come unbidden now...
they make me feel
hello my world...i see your back again

but events happened to bring them
out infront of everyone
made me look crazy...no one
understood...they were afraid
me...i was terrified at what i coule no
longer control or hide
hello my world...i see your back again

Hello My World
-continued-

i lost myself...i lost everything i held
dear and i didnt know why
years of searching for an answer of
what was wrong with me
after ten years...i had my answer...i
could deal with my affliction
hello my world...i see your back again

my story is told...my pain revisited and
felt...told to strangers
the only ones who seem to listen and
feel my words and pain
the only ones who may be objective to
my plight and befriend me
hello my world...i see your back again

unfortunately...no one else wanted to
deal with me...i withdrew
living in my shell for protection from a
careless word or deed
pushing others away so i didnt hurt as
much...but i still do
hello my world...i see your back again

Days Are Gone
-for momma-who passed from alzheimers in 2004-

days past long ago when she walked with me
when i could reach deep into her soul and see her
seeing her as she used to be...my mother...my friend
those days are gone...my time with her is past

bridging the gap between her and me was hard
seeing her slip into that abyss of her world
filled my heart with sadness...yet for a time we were one
those days are gone...my time with her is past

letting her be herself...yet letting her know i was there
held a richness all its own...i lost a mother...but gained a friend
sharing our short time together...just her and me
those days are gone...my time with her is past

she gave me a whole lifetime...hers and mine
though i feel her loss...i treasure her memories forever
alzheimers will never take those away from me
those days are gone...my time with her is past

Fury
-written by my granddaughter, Adrienne, at 13-

Fury

written by my granddaughter, Adrienne, at age 13

He struck her face with flashing anger
Leaving her burned, scarred, shocked
He blazed with electrifying fury
More raps, with the same spark of madness
Thunder shook all around them
In the wake of his rampage
And the storm clouds glided away, taking him with them
Lightening threatened to return
But Mother Earth can take it
The craters will heal
The trees will grow back
And Lightening will return
Because he always does

For Who I Am

i am the sum total of who i am
i have become who i am from my experiences
i am who i have become by what i've seen
i am who i am by the thoughts within my mind
i am what people have made me to be
for who i am comes from my life

www.ingramcontent.com/pod-product-compliance
Lightning Source LLC
Chambersburg PA
CBHW041701160426
43191CB00002B/46